BASEBALL

RECORDS

BY ALLAN MOREY

BLASTOFF!
DISCOVERY

Blastoff! Discovery launches
a new mission: reading to learn.
Filled with facts and features,
each book offers you an exciting
new world to explore!

This edition first published in 2018 by Bellwether Media, Inc.

No part of this publication may be reproduced in whole or in
part without written permission of the publisher.
For information regarding permission, write to Bellwether
Media, Inc., Attention: Permissions Department,
5357 Penn Avenue South, Minneapolis, MN 55419.

Library of Congress Cataloging-in-Publication Data

Names: Morey, Allan, author.
Title: Baseball Records / by Allan Morey.
Description: Minneapolis, MN : Bellwether Media, Inc., 2018. |
    Series: Blastoff! Discovery. Incredible Sports Records | Includes
    bibliographical references and index. | Audience: Age 7-13.
    | Audience: Grade 3 to 8.
Identifiers: LCCN 2017032153 (print) | LCCN
    2017032982 (ebook) | ISBN 9781626177819
    (hardcover : alk. paper) | ISBN 9781618913111 (pbk. : alk.
    paper) | ISBN 9781681034928 (ebook)
Subjects: LCSH: Baseball–Records–United States–Juvenile
    literature. | Major League Baseball–Juvenile literature.
Classification: LCC GV877 (ebook) | LCC GV877 .M67 2018
    (print) | DDC 796.357/6406–dc23
LC record available at https://lccn.loc.gov/2017032153

Editor: Nathan Sommer   Designer: Steve Porter

Printed in the United States of America, North Mankato, MN.

TABLE OF CONTENTS

RECORD-BREAKING STREAK

It is September 6, 1995. Baltimore Orioles fans erupt into cheers as the game ends. Their team won, but they are really cheering for star **shortstop** Cal Ripken, Jr. He just broke the Major League Baseball (MLB) record by playing his 2,131st game in a row.

Ripken went on to extend this amazing
streak, playing in 2,632 **consecutive** games.
His MLB record is just one of many feats that
have amazed fans over the years. Read on to
learn about other incredible MLB records.

RECORD-BREAKING PLAYERS

Professional baseball has been around since 1876. During this time, many great pitchers have flung the ball toward **home plate**. Just as many powerful hitters have stepped up to bat.

Barry Bonds is a major **offensive** player in baseball history. In 2001, he set the record for most **home runs** in a single season with 73. Bonds ended his career with a record 762 home runs.

BALLPARK BARRY

Barry Bonds holds the record for most career runs batted in with 2,297.

MOST CAREER HOME RUNS

Record: 762 home runs
Record holder: Barry Bonds
Year record was set: 2007
Former record holder:
Hank Aaron

Pitcher Cy Young won a staggering 511 games during his career. His record is truly unbeatable. Only one other pitcher has won more than 400 games. No wonder the award given to the best MLB pitchers every year is named after Young!

MOST CAREER WINS

Record: 511 wins
Record holder: Cy Young
Year record was set: 1911
Former record holder:
Pud Galvin

Rickey Henderson is one of the fastest MLB players ever. He set records with his speed. Henderson once stole a record 130 bases in one season. He retired with an unbelievable career record of 1,406 **stolen bases**.

No one was better at striking out opposing hitters than Nolan Ryan. He struck out 5,714 batters during his 27-year career. He has over 800 more **strikeouts** than all other pitchers!

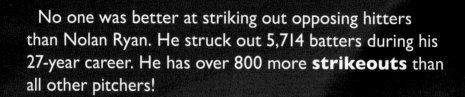

NO-HITTERS

Ryan also holds the record for most no-hitters thrown. He did this seven different times, three more times than the next best pitcher.

MOST CAREER STRIKEOUTS

Record: 5,714 strikeouts
Record holder: Nolan Ryan
Year record was set: 1993
Former record holder:
Walter Johnson

MOST CAREER SAVES

Record: 652 saves
Record holder: Mariano Rivera
Year record was set: 2013
Former record holder:
Trevor Hoffman

Closers come in at the end of the game to stop opposing hitters from tying or winning the game. Mariano Rivera made a career as a closing pitcher for the New York Yankees. His 652 career **saves** remain the most in MLB history!

MLB legend Joe DiMaggio had his record 45th consecutive game with a hit on July 2, 1941. But he did not stop there. He extended the record to 56 straight games! More than 70 years later, no one has come close to challenging DiMaggio's record.

ON BASE

Ted Williams holds the record for getting on base in the most consecutive games. He had a hit or was walked in 84 straight games!

MOST CONSECUTIVE GAMES WITH A HIT

Record: 56
Record holder: Joe DiMaggio
Year record was set: 1941
Former record holder:
Willie Keeler

MOST HITS IN A SEASON

Record: 262 hits
Record holder: Ichiro Suzuki
Year record was set: 2004
Former record holder:
George Sisler

Ichiro Suzuki sent the ball flying during his last at bat on October 1, 2004. The hit, his 258th of the season, broke the MLB record for most hits in a season. Suzuki went on to end the season with a spectacular 262 hits!

RECORD-BREAKING TEAMS

MLB teams depend on both talent and teamwork to win. When a group of players works well together, amazing things can happen.

Many consider the New York Yankees the most dominant baseball team in history. They have made it to the World Series a record 40 times. Their unbelievable 27 World Series wins are an MLB record!

COMMISSIONER'S TROPHY

The winner of the World Series receives the Commissioner's Trophy.

WORLD SERIES CHAMPIONSHIPS WON

Record: 27 World Series
Record holder: New York Yankees
Year record was set: 2009
Former record holder:
St. Louis Cardinals

The 2001 Seattle Mariners tied a record that had stood for nearly 100 years. That season, they won a historic 116 games on their way to a **playoff** appearance. This matched the record number of wins set by the 1906 Chicago Cubs.

MOST WINS IN A SEASON

Record: 116 wins
Record holders: Chicago Cubs (1906) and Seattle Mariners (2001)
Year record was set: first set in 1906
Former record holder:
New York Giants

OLDEST ACTIVE BASEBALL FRANCHISE

Record holder: Atlanta Braves
Year record was set: 1871
Previous record holder: N/A

Founded in 1903, the MLB is one of the oldest professional sports leagues in the world. Some **franchises** have been around since before the league even existed. The Atlanta Braves started playing as the Boston Red Stockings in 1871. They are the oldest active franchise in baseball!

SECOND-OLDEST

The Chicago Cubs are the second-oldest active franchise in the MLB. They have been around since 1874.

The Cleveland Indians made magic happen during the 2017 season. The team powered its way to 22 straight victories, the longest win streak in **American League** history. The team outscored opponents 142–37 during this spectacular hot streak!

LONGEST UNBEATEN STREAK

In 1916, the New York Giants played 26 games in a row without a loss. MLB considers this the league's longest win streak. However, some people disagree since one game ended in a tie.

LONGEST WIN STREAK, AMERICAN LEAGUE

Record: 22 games

Record holder: Cleveland Indians

Year record was set: 2017

Former record holder:
Oakland Athletics

MOST HOME RUNS BY A TEAM, SINGLE-SEASON

Record: 264 home runs
Record holder: Seattle Mariners
Year record was set: 1997
Former record holder:
Baltimore Orioles

The 1997 Seattle Mariners team was full of big hitters. Superstars like Ken Griffey Jr. and Alex Rodriguez prepared the team for success from game one. The team ended up hitting a record 264 home runs that season!

RECORD-BREAKING GAMES

The average baseball game is nine **innings** and lasts about three hours. But when a game is tied at nine innings, extra innings are added to decide a winner. Games like these may end up breaking records!

On August 25, 1922, the Chicago Cubs and Philadelphia Phillies broke an important record. They combined for a record 49 **runs** before the Cubs took the victory! Usually, there are only about 8 runs in an MLB game.

MOST TOTAL RUNS SCORED IN A GAME

Record: 49
Record holders: Chicago Cubs and
Philadelphia Phillies
Year record was set: 1922
Former record holders:
New York Giants and Cincinnati Reds

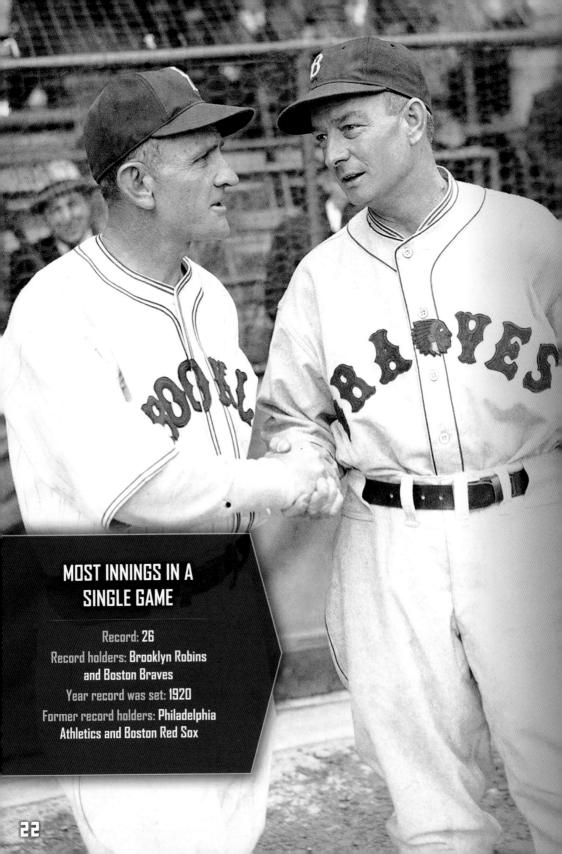

MOST INNINGS IN A SINGLE GAME

Record: 26
Record holders: Brooklyn Robins
and Boston Braves
Year record was set: 1920
Former record holders: Philadelphia
Athletics and Boston Red Sox

The Brooklyn Robins and Boston Braves played a game that refused to end on May 1, 1920. The game took a record 26 innings to finish! The teams stayed tied 1–1 until darkness forced the game to end.

Fans were patient when the Milwaukee Brewers and Chicago White Sox faced off on May 8, 1984. The game went 25 innings and lasted a record 8 hours and 6 minutes. The Sox beat the Brewers 7–6 to end this longest game in MLB history!

LONGEST MLB GAME

Record: 8 hours, 6 minutes
Record holders: Milwaukee Brewers
and Chicago White Sox
Year record was set: 1984

Batters from the Chicago Cubs and New York Yankees struggled to hit on May 7, 2017. Pitchers from both teams combined for a record 48 strikeouts! The game lasted 18 innings before the Yankees won 5–4.

MOST COMBINED STRIKEOUTS IN A GAME

Record: 48 strikeouts
Record holders: Chicago Cubs and New York Yankees
Year record was set: 2017
Former record holders: Los Angeles Angels and Oakland Athletics

The Chicago White Sox and Detroit Tigers put on a show for fans on May 28, 1995. The teams combined for a record 12 home runs that day. Oddly, these same two teams tied this record again on July 2, 2002!

MOST COMBINED HOME RUNS IN A GAME

Record: 12
Record holders: Chicago White Sox and Detroit Tigers
Year record was set: first set in 1995
Former record holders: eight teams

RECORD-BREAKING PLAYS

History can be made in a split second during an MLB game. In one play, a player might hit the farthest home run or launch the fastest pitch. Fans never know what to expect!

There is much debate over who has hit the longest home run. Home run distance was not properly tracked until 2009. Since then, Aaron Judge has smashed the farthest one. His home run on June 11, 2017 traveled 496 feet (151 meters)!

THE STUFF OF LEGENDS

Babe Ruth and Mickey Mantle were both said to have hit home runs over 600 feet (183 meters). Sadly, historians cannot prove the exact distances.

LONGEST HOME RUN
SINCE 2009

Record: 496 feet (151 meters)
Record holder: Aaron Judge
Year record was set: 2017
Former record holders:
two players

FASTEST PITCH

Record: 105.1 miles
(169.1 kilometers) per hour
Record holder: Aroldis Chapman
Year record was set: 2010
Former record holder:
Joel Zumaya

Aroldis Chapman pitched his way into the record books on
September 24, 2010. That day, he threw multiple **fastballs**
faster than 100 miles (161 kilometers) per hour. One reached

Miami Marlins player Giancarlo Stanton has crushed the ball since joining the MLB. On June 9, 2016, he hit harder than ever before. That day, Stanton's massive hit clocked in at a record 123.9 miles (199.3 kilometers) per hour!

FASTEST HIT

Record: 123.9 miles
(199.3 kilometers) per hour
Record holder: Giancarlo Stanton
Year record was set: 2016
Former record holder:
broke his own record

GLOSSARY

American League—one of the two major leagues that make up the MLB; the other is the National League.

closers—pitchers who typically pitch the final outs of a game

consecutive—one right after the other

fastballs—pitches thrown at full speed

franchises—teams that are members of a professional sports league

home plate—the rubber base where batters stand to hit the ball; runners must also touch home plate to score.

home runs—hits that allow a batter to go around all four bases and score a run; typically, home runs occur when a batter knocks the ball over the outfield wall.

innings—parts of a baseball game during which each team gets to bat until they have three outs; most baseball games have nine innings.

offensive—relating to the player or team that has the ball and is trying to score, such as the batters and runners in baseball

playoff—games played after the regular season is over; MLB playoff games determine which teams play in the World Series.

runs—points scored in a baseball game; runs are gained when a player rounds all three bases and returns to home plate.

saves—a stat that pitchers earn; pitchers most often earn saves at the end of the game by stopping the opposing team from tying or winning the game.

shortstop—an infielder positioned between second and third base

stolen bases—plays in which a runner advances from one base to another without the baseball being put into play by the batter

streak—a series of events that happen one right after the other

strikeouts—outs caused by a pitcher getting three called strikes against a batter

TO LEARN MORE

AT THE LIBRARY

Chandler, Matt. *Wacky Baseball Trivia: Fun Facts for Every Fan.*
North Mankato, Minn.: Capstone Press, 2017.

Savage, Jeff. *Baseball Super Stats.* Minneapolis, Minn.: Lerner
Publications, 2018.

Scheff, Matt. *Incredible Baseball Records.* Mankato, Minn.:
Child's World, 2016.

ON THE WEB

Learning more about baseball records
is as easy as 1, 2, 3.

1. Go to www.factsurfer.com.

2. Enter "baseball records" into the search box.

3. Click the "Surf" button and you will see a list of related web sites.

With factsurfer.com, finding more information is just a click away.

INDEX

The images in this book are reproduced through the courtesy of: Ron Vesely/ Getty Images, front cover, p. 10; GARY HERSHORN/ REUTERS/ Newscom, p. 4; David Durochik/ AP Images, pp. 5, 9; Scott Troyanos/ Getty Images, pp. 6-7; Transcendental Graphics/ Getty Images, p. 8; Eugene Parciasepe, p. 11; Bettmann/ Getty Images, p. 12; JOHN FROSCHAUER/ AP Images, p. 13; Kathy Willens/ AP Images, pp. 14-15; Otto Greule Jr/ Getty Images, p. 16; FPG/ Getty Images, p. 17; John Sleezer/ ZUMA Press, p. 18; Jim Ruymen UPI Photo Service/ Newscom, p. 19; Chicago History Museum/ ZUMA Press, pp. 20-21; AP Images, pp. 22-23; David Banks/ Getty Images, p. 24; The Sporting News/ Getty Images, p. 25; JT Vintage/ ZUMA Press, p. 26 (small); Mike Stobe/ Getty Images, pp. 26-27; Christian Petersen/ Getty Images, p. 28; David Santiago/ AP Images, p. 29.